TERRORIST
DOSSIERS

# JIHAD

## Islamic Fundamentalist
## TERRORISM

# Samuel M. KATZ

Lerner Publications Company/Minneapolis

To the NYPD and PAPD heroes who raced into
the fires of hell on 9/11 and whose courage
enabled so many thousands to survive
—SMK

Publisher's Note: The information in this book was current at the time of publication. However, the
publisher is aware that news involving current events dates quickly. Please refer to the websites on
page 69 for places to go to obtain up-to-date information.

Lerner Publications Company
A division of Lerner Publishing Group
241 First Avenue North
Minneapolis, Minnesota U.S.A.

Website address: www.lernerbooks.com

Library of Congress Cataloging-in-Publication Data

Katz, Samuel M., 1963–
        Jihad: Islamic fundamentalist terrorism / by Samuel M. Katz.
            p.    cm. — (Terrorist dossiers)
        Includes bibliographical references and index.
        Contents: Introduction – The history of Islam and fundamentalism – The fire is kindled: Egypt's
Jihad warriors – Deadly force: Lebanon's Hezbollah – Unchecked wrath: Algeria's Groupe
Islamique Armé – Global terror: Al-Qaeda's international network.
        ISBN: 0–8225–4031–2 (lib. bdg. : alk. paper)
        1. Jihad. 2. Islamic fundamentalism. 3. Terrorism—Religious aspects—Islam. [1. Jihad.
2. Islamic fundamentalism. 3. Terrorism—Religious aspects—Islam.] I. Title.
BP182.K37 2004
303.6'25'0882971—dc21                                                              2003005626

Manufactured in the United States of America
1 2 3 4 5 6 – DP – 09 08 07 06 05 04

# CONTENTS

**Algerian government:** supported by France and operating from Algiers, a secular authority that has traditionally resisted Islamic leadership. Many have accused the Algerian government of being deeply corrupt and of participating in the violence of a civil war that raged throughout the 1990s.

**Abdullah Yusuf Azzam:** a Palestinian cleric who organized Arab resistance fighters (mujahideen) during the Afghan-Soviet War. Azzam and Osama bin Laden would later work as partners in the global jihad.

**Hasan al-Banna:** the founder and early leader of the Muslim Brotherhood Society

**Osama bin Laden:** the founder and commander of al-Qaeda. Bin Laden and Abdullah Azzam worked together to organize the Afghan resistance to the Soviet invasion.

**C.E.:** Middle Eastern history spans both ancient and modern times. To refer to historical dates, some books use the abbreviation A.D. (*anno Domini*, or "in the year of the Lord"). This dating system is based on the birth of Jesus. This book uses the abbreviation C.E., or "of the common era," instead of A.D.

**Egyptian government:** operating from Cairo, a secular government that has repressed Islamic fundamentalist movements, both political and terrorist in nature

**Sheikh Mohammed Hussein Fadlallah:** one of the founders and first leaders of the terrorist group Hezbollah

**Front Islamique du Salut, or Islamic Salvation Front (FIS):**
Algeria's first and most prominent Islamic political party

**al-Gamaa al-Islamiya:** an underground Islamic fundamentalist
terrorist group founded in Egypt in about 1973. It seeks the
establishment of an Islamic state in Egypt.

**Groupe Islamique Armé, or Armed Islamic Group (GIA):**
a terrorist group with the goal of establishing an Islamic
government in Algeria. During Algeria's long civil war in
the 1990s, the GIA carried out civilian massacres as well
as targeting foreigners and government officials.

**Hezbollah:** a Shiite terrorist group based in Lebanon.
Supported by Syria and Iraq, Hezbollah seeks an Islamic
government in Lebanon. The group is also active in the
Palestinian-Israeli conflict.

**Islam:** a religion founded on the Arabian Peninsula in the
seventh century C.E. by the prophet Muhammad. Most followers
of Islam, called Muslims, are members of the Sunni sect,
while other Muslims follow the stricter Shiite branch of the
religion.

**Islamic fundamentalism:** a school of thought that supports
the return to traditional Islamic ideals and government and
that opposes Western influence on the Islamic world. Most
Islamic fundamentalists do not advocate terrorism.

**jihad:** an Arabic word meaning "holy struggle" or "holy war."
Some Islamic fundamentalists see the jihad as a violent
fight against Western and non-Islamic influence.

**al-Jihad:** an Egyptian Islamic fundamentalist terrorist group founded in the late 1960s. Also known as Egyptian Islamic Jihad, al-Jihad's goal is to replace Egypt's secular government with an Islamic one.

**Ayatollah Khomeini:** a Shiite cleric who took power in Iran after its Islamic revolution in 1979. Khomeini died in 1989.

**Lebanese government:** operating from Beirut and traditionally a coalition government comprised of representatives from Lebanon's many ethnic and religious groups. Sunni Muslims and Maronite Christians have tended to hold the most powerful positions in the Lebanese government.

**the Middle East:** a geographical and political term that usually refers to nations in eastern North Africa and southwestern Asia

**Imad Mughniyah:** commander of Hezbollah's terrorist operations arm, the Special Security Apparatus. Mughniyah played a large role in introducing suicide bombing to modern Islamic fundamentalist terrorism.

**mujahideen:** Afghan resistance fighters. The mujahideen fought the Soviets during their occupation of Afghanistan. Most mujahideen are devout Muslims.

**Muslim Brotherhood Society:** an Islamic fundamentalist group formed in Egypt in 1928 by the cleric Hasan al-Banna. Although the brotherhood began as a political party, it eventually developed terrorist offshoots.

**al-Qaeda:** an Islamic fundamentalist terrorist group founded in about 1989 and commanded by Osama bin Laden. Al-Qaeda's goal is a global jihad uniting Islamic movements around the world.

**Quran:** the holy book of Islam. According to Islamic belief, the Quran's teachings were communicated by Allah (God) to the prophet Muhammad. These divine messages were later collected and recorded in a single volume, originally written in Arabic.

**Sheikh Omar Abdel Rahman:** an influential Islamic cleric who was a leader in the Muslim Brotherhood and later moved to the United States, where he continued to preach

**re-Islamization:** a tenet of Islamic fundamentalist thought. Supporters of re-Islamization believe that problems in the Islamic world are due to the Western-influenced movement away from traditional Islamic ideals and that the solution is to return to those ideals.

**Sharia:** Islamic law. Most of Sharia's rules are derived from the Quran, but various Muslim sects and governments interpret and apply Sharia differently.

**Taliban:** a very strict Islamic fundamentalist government that held power in Afghanistan from 1996 to 2001 and that supported and protected Osama bin Laden and al-Qaeda

**the West:** a geographic and political term that usually refers to the United States and western Europe

**Westernization:** a process, favored by some Islamic politicians and leaders, of seeking the equality of the Islamic world with the Western world. "Westernizers" believe that Islamic nations should be open to the political, economic, and cultural practices of the West.

# INTRODUCTION

The footage is unforgettable. Its significance is devastating. On the morning of September 11, 2001, low-flying planes moving at incredible speed struck the twin towers of the World Trade Center in New York City. Within minutes television stations around the world were broadcasting the news to thousands of people who watched in horror. Two terrible hours later, both towers—symbols of U.S. economic power since their construction in the 1970s—had collapsed. Two hundred miles away, smoke poured out of a gaping hole in the wall of the Pentagon, headquarters of the U.S. military. And in a remote Pennsylvania field, the charred remains of a plane lay smoldering on the ground.

The twin towers burn after being struck by the terrorist attacks of September 11.

Close to three thousand people died that day in the largest terrorist strike ever to take place on U.S. soil. As the rescue and recovery operations began at Ground Zero, as the former site of the towers came to be called, investigation of the attacks began. In the next few days, some Americans heard for the first time the names Osama bin Laden and al-Qaeda. The details were still murky, but one thing was all too clear. The United States had been singled out for one of the most brutal and tragic attacks in history by one of the most deadly and powerful terrorist networks in the world. The terrorists' goal was to carry out a ruthless struggle against all those whom they saw as enemies of Islam. They called this struggle the jihad.

Throughout history, suspicion, fear, and hatred have plagued relationships between Islamic nations and the West. In the twentieth century, fundamentalist Islam—a movement that strives to restore traditional Islamic ideals—became a powerful force in the Islamic and Arab world. Especially following the creation of the Jewish State of Israel in 1948, radical elements of this movement have taken it to a new level by introducing terrorism.

Bent on the destruction of non-Muslims and the West—or at least the expulsion of Western influence from the Islamic world—fundamentalist Islamic terrorist groups have carried out horrific attacks. From the emergence of violent fundamentalist groups in Egypt, to a ruthless civil war in Algeria, to the destruction of September 11, this bloody terrorist campaign has wrought death and damage that have forever changed the world. And even as the painful rebuilding takes place at Ground Zero, the terror continues.

# THE HISTORY OF ISLAM AND FUNDAMENTALISM

Those who have committed acts of terrorism in the name of Islam have given it an unjust reputation as a religion of violence and hatred. In fact, Islam is a rich, multifaceted faith with a long and magnificent past. It is one of the world's three major monotheistic (one-god) religions, along with Judaism and Christianity. Islam has nearly one billion followers, called Muslims, who live in nations around the world.

**BEGINNINGS** Islam's roots can be traced back to 570 C.E., when Muhammad, the religion's founder, was born in the town of Mecca. Mecca was a major trading post on the Arabian Peninsula, and Muhammad was a merchant by profession. Mecca was also a center for the ancient pagan religions that most Arabs of the time practiced. According to Islamic tradition, Muhammad received a revelation from God in about 610, bidding him to begin spreading the word of a new religion. This new faith, Islam, focused on devotion and submission to one god, called Allah in Arabic. Allah, Muhammad preached, had sent a series of prophets to earth, ranging from Moses to Jesus and ending with Muhammad himself. Throughout the centuries, said Muhammad, these religious messengers had delivered a system of laws and religious requirements, such as those in the Jewish Torah and the Christian Bible. Muslims believe that these messages culminated in the Quran, Islam's holy book.

The rise of Islam was slow at first. Muhammad's preaching was not well received in his native Mecca. The locals—particularly the town's wealthiest residents—had no wish to be converted to the new faith of this young merchant. Mecca was a center for the region's main religion.

# THE FAITH

Islam is subdivided into many sects. The two most prominent are the Sunnis, who comprise nearly 90 percent of the world's Muslims, and the stricter Shiites, who live primarily in Iran, Iraq, and Lebanon. Other sects include the Druze of Lebanon and Syria and the mostly Syrian Alawites.

The Quran holds Muhammad's divine revelations. Because Muslims believe that the word of Allah was directly recorded in the Quran, devout Muslims in all nations must learn to read the original Arabic text. The Quran—along with descriptions of Muhammad's sayings and actions, written by his followers—provides Muslims with guidance in nearly every aspect of life. For example, the texts set forth rules regarding diet, marriage, money matters, and law. Islamic law, called Sharia, defines crimes and punishments.

Every year more than one million Muslims make the hajj to Mecca. Many pray before the Kaaba at the Grand Mosque *(above)*.

One of the Quran's major contributions to Islamic life is a set of religious duties that all Muslims must perform and upon which Islam is built. Called the five pillars of Islam, these duties are *shahada* (the declaration of faith), *salat* (prayer), *zakat* (charity), *sawm* (fasting), and *hajj* (pilgrimage) to the holy city of Mecca, which all Muslims must try to make once in their lifetime.

Some of these duties, such as prayer, are performed daily. Muslims pray five times each day at home and in mosques (Islamic places of worship). Other pillars are acted out only at certain times of the year. For example, Muslims fast during the holy month of Ramadan. Ramadan ends with Eid al-Fitr, a great festival and feast.

Another important Islamic concept is jihad, meaning "holy struggle." Often a jihad is the personal struggle to overcome the evil that is within oneself or in one's life and to conquer it with good. For others jihad can have political overtones. ■

Meccan traders and rulers gained much of their wealth from business with the many pilgrims who came to view the city's sacred sites. Muhammad was eventually forced out of Mecca in 622. He fled to the nearby town of Medina, which would become the second holiest city in Islam after Mecca.

| A GREAT EMPIRE | By the time of Muhammad's death in 632, he had laid the foundations of the world's first Islamic state. He had also begun the expansion of that state. In the mid- to late seventh century, armies of Islamic soldiers swept across the Middle East, the Arab world, and beyond, establishing an Islamic Empire that covered large portions of Asia, Africa, and Europe. Eventually, the empire extended from the Atlantic Ocean in the west to the Indus River in the east. Over the centuries, capitals were established in cities including Damascus, Syria; Baghdad, Iraq; and Seville, Spain.

As the religion expanded, Islamic art, architecture, literature, law, and science also spread throughout the empire. At the same time, as the

The Islamic Empire extended as far north as Cordoba, Spain, where this mosque still stands as a striking example of Islamic architecture.

empire absorbed new areas and peoples, it adopted many of the best features of these new cultures. The realm consequently grew in diversity as well as in size and strength. But the great empire's unifying force remained Islam. Religion guided nearly every facet of life, society, and proper behavior and was seen as inseparable from government.

Islamic power did not go completely unchallenged. The empire's leaders, called caliphs, faced resistance to their conquest and rule in regions such as northern Spain. But a far greater threat came from within the massive caliphate (Islamic Empire), as individual kingdoms and rulers sprang up to challenge the caliphs' overarching control.

Within the empire's control was Jerusalem and the surrounding area of what would become Israel. This region, often called the Holy Land, is sacred to Judaism, Christianity, and Islam as the site of important events in the histories of all three religions. In the eleventh century, the area's unique and far-reaching value became the source of a new threat to the caliphate. Christian warriors from Europe launched the Crusades, a series of invasions and wars that took place between 1096 and 1270 in the Middle East. The Crusaders' goal was to capture the Holy Land from the Islamic Empire and to claim Jerusalem for Christianity. To Muslims, though, the long and violent Crusades seemed like an attempt by Christianity to crush Islam and to dominate its people.

Crusaders invade the Holy Land, attempting to bring it under Christian rule.

The Crusades ultimately failed, and the region remained under Muslim control, although it was not unified under a single ruler. Smaller sub-empires emerged, the most important of which was the Ottoman Empire. The Ottoman Empire began in the 1300s in the region that would later become Turkey. In the fifteenth and sixteenth centuries, the Ottomans captured vast holdings in North Africa and the Middle East.

Ottoman rulers also challenged European power, conquering areas as far west as modern-day Hungary. But by the 1600s, the empire's hold in Europe had weakened. By the nineteenth century, European states including Britain, France, Italy, and Russia had begun to threaten Ottoman territory in North Africa and Asia. These European nations established varying degrees of control in Algeria, Egypt, Tunisia, Morocco, Iran, and Iraq.

Nevertheless, the weakened Ottoman Empire held together into the early twentieth century. When World War I began in 1914, the Ottomans joined the conflict on the side of the Central Powers, alongside Germany and Austria-Hungary. They faced the Allies,

Ottoman rulers such as Suleyman *(center, on horse)* held power over a vast Islamic realm.

which included Britain, the United States, France, and Russia. When the Central Powers were defeated in 1918, the Allies divided the Ottoman Empire among themselves, creating individual states out of the realm and installing leaders of their choosing. The region's people—most of whom were Muslims—suddenly found themselves governed, directly or indirectly, by European and primarily Christian powers.

## THE GROWTH OF ZIONISM

One of the areas carved out of the Ottoman Empire was the British mandate of Palestine, which included Jerusalem and the core of the Holy Land. Tensions were already high there, due to a steady stream of Jewish immigrants seeking to escape anti-Semitism (anti-Jewish prejudice) in Europe. These new settlers were Zionists, supporters of a political movement to establish a Jewish state in

British soldiers respond to Arab protests and violence in Jerusalem.

the Holy Land. During and after World War II (1939–1945) and the Holocaust, in which the German Nazis killed six million European Jews, Jewish immigration to Palestine surged. The call for a Jewish state grew louder. Local Palestinians, uneasy about the prospect of becoming a minority in their home country, opposed immigration ever more vehemently. They also opposed British power—sometimes violently.

Hoping to resolve the issue, the United Nations (a newly formed organization handling international disputes) issued a plan to partition, or divide, the land. British power over the region would end on May 14, 1948. The area would then be split into two independent states: one for the Jews and one for the Palestinians.

Palestinians and the rest of the Arab world were against the plan, unwilling to allow outside powers to divide and control their territory. May 14 arrived. The Jewish State of Israel was declared. The next day, Arab forces from Egypt, Iraq, Syria, Jordan, Lebanon, Yemen, Saudi Arabia, and Palestine itself invaded the new nation.

The Arab troops were thousands strong and expected a quick and easy victory over Israel. Instead, they experienced a crushing and humiliating loss. That defeat would be repeated in another Arab-Israeli war in 1967 and yet another in 1973. Over the course of these wars, as

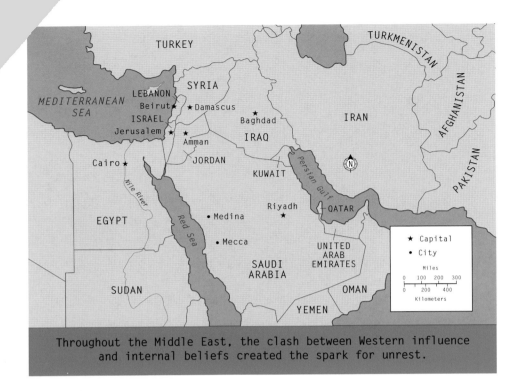

Throughout the Middle East, the clash between Western influence and internal beliefs created the spark for unrest.

Israel increased its territory and no independent Palestinian state emerged, the issue became a source of tremendous bitterness for Arabs throughout the Middle East. Their hostility was directed not only at Israel but also at its supporters—one of the strongest and most vocal of which was the United States. To many Arab Muslims, it seemed that, from the Crusades to partition, contact between their world and that of the West had led only to misery.

## | OIL |

Of course, while there was cause for unrest in the region, not everyone lived in despair. Vast reserves of oil had been discovered in Saudi Arabia, Iraq, and other Middle Eastern countries in the early 1900s. This precious resource yielded tremendous wealth, which expanded even further during an oil boom in the 1970s. But that wealth was enjoyed by only a privileged few, who drove expensive cars, built luxurious homes, and wore fancy clothes.

Along with wealth, power was unevenly shared in the Arab world. Many of the states in the Middle East and North Africa were harsh dictatorships and monarchies. Leaders ruled absolutely, often with little regard for the welfare and civil rights of their people.

Oil riches, the Palestinian-Israeli conflict, and the lack of democracy and personal freedom throughout the Muslim world fed the silent rage felt by millions. To some, it seemed that their best hope for salvation was their religion. Seeking guidance, they turned to the Quran and the mosques.

## THE RISE OF FUNDAMENTALISM | By the twentieth

century, hundreds of years of friction had led to deep misunderstanding, mistrust, fear, and, for some, hatred of the West in Islamic society. Fears of Christian or Jewish domination influenced the leaders of some Arab states. To the masses, the wealth, power, and prestige of Western nations stood in striking contrast to the desperate poverty, hunger, lack of education, and lack of political influence faced by all but an elite few in the Islamic world. What had happened, they wondered, to the glory and the power of the Islamic Empire?

Some Muslims felt that the best way to achieve the status and privileges enjoyed by Western nations was to adopt Western ways. These "Westernizers" claimed that Islamic nations could gain equal footing with the West by following its political, economic, and cultural practices.

But to others, it seemed that the only answer was "re-Islamization." The problems that the Islamic world faced, they believed, were due to the movement away from traditional Islamic ideals—a

The desperate poverty of so many in the Muslim world, such as these Egyptian *zabaleen* ("garbage people"), was a factor in the growth of the Islamic fundamentalist movement.

movement largely caused by Western influence. The only way to recapture the glory of the past was to return to those ideals.

At first, Westernization won more followers than re-Islamization. But as Muslims living under Westernized governments continued to see little improvement in their lives, a drive to restore the basics—the fundamentals—of Islam grew stronger and stronger. Islamic values and morals were being eroded by Westernization, they declared. Even governments in the region that claimed to be Islamic were often on friendly terms with Western governments. The West, many felt, was a corrupting influence that had to be driven from Islamic society.

These Islamic fundamentalists began setting up community organizations to aid the poor, the illiterate, the hungry, and the sick. Through these services, they established a broad base of support among the common people of Arab nations. That support, they hoped, would eventually lead to the creation of governments founded on Islam. These governments were the only ones, in the fundamentalist view, that could effectively and responsibly lead Muslim populations.

As the Islamic fundamentalist movement took shape, the vast majority of its followers opposed violence and terrorism. They wanted only to live in a unified Islamic world free of Western control. But as time went on, some fundamentalists wanted to take the movement to a new level. For them, the valued Islamic idea of the jihad came to have the new meaning of violent, armed struggle—a holy war—between the Islamic world and the West. The soldiers of this new jihad were terrorists, willing to sacrifice innocent lives for their cause.

# THE FIRE IS KINDLED:
# EGYPT'S JIHAD WARRIORS

**W**ith a history of power dating back to the pyramids and the pharaohs, Egypt was once the undisputed leader of the Arab world. But by the twentieth century, Egypt was having its share of problems. Occupied first by the Ottoman Turks and then by the British Empire, Egypt gained independence in 1922. However, the monarchy that took power in the postcolonial period was deeply corrupt. Islamic fundamentalism emerged as an answer to foreign occupation and a quest for the empowerment of ordinary citizens. The new fundamentalist revolution thrived in Egyptian universities and mosques.

The movement took a more concrete shape in 1928, when the fiery cleric Hasan al-Banna founded the Muslim Brotherhood Society in Ismailia, Egypt. Al-Banna sought to build a powerful political party that would fight for the liberation of Egypt from Western and non-Islamic control. Imams (prayer leaders) and other Islamic figures lectured about the glorious history of the Arab world and

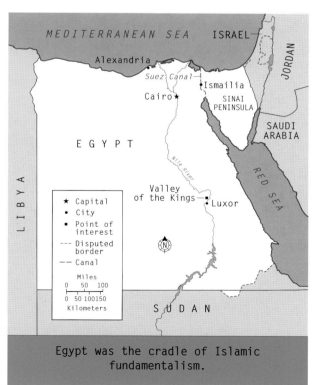

Egypt was the cradle of Islamic fundamentalism.

Muslim Brotherhood members gather in Cairo to listen to an imam (Muslim cleric).

of Islam's great victories. Mosques offered the poor and the powerless comfort and answers. The imams condemned political corruption and oppression in secular Arab nations as evils caused by ties to the West and declared that these foreign influences were unacceptable to devout Muslims.

As the brotherhood's power increased and its calls for change grew louder, radical members of the group began taking stronger action, targeting British troops still stationed in Egypt with hit-and-run attacks. These terrorists' ultimate goal was the establishment of an Egyptian Islamic state, which would then serve as proof that other Arab nations could overthrow their Westernized regimes and replace them with Islamic governments.

## RISE AND REPRESSION | The pivotal event that

transformed the Muslim Brotherhood into a violent force was the creation of Israel in 1948. Following the subsequent Arab-Israeli War, feelings of bitter humiliation flooded the mosques of Cairo, Egypt's capital. Outraged brotherhood members blamed Egypt's King Farouk and his pro-Western stance for the catastrophic Arab defeat. They began to openly call for a revolution that would bring Islamic rule to Egypt. Then, on December 28, 1948, brotherhood gunmen assassinated King Farouk's prime minister, Mahmud Fahmi Nokrashi. King Farouk's secret police, the Mukhabarat, responded with equal force, assassinating Hasan al-Banna in Cairo a year later.

Al-Banna's death was a serious blow to the brotherhood, and the group retreated for the time being to a more religious and less political focus. In 1951 Hasan al-Hudaybi, a moderate fundamentalist, took leadership of the group. But political unrest still simmered below the surface.

In 1952 Colonel Gamal Abdel Nasser seized control of Egypt in a military coup (swift takeover). Viewing the powerful brotherhood as a potential threat to his own authority, Nasser outlawed the group and rounded up activists. The Muslim Brotherhood responded with renewed fury, launching several unsuccessful assassination attempts against Nasser. He, in turn, vowed to crush the movement. In 1966 Nasser ordered the execution of Sayyid Qutb, one of the brotherhood's leaders. Others would soon face the same fate, Nasser promised.

Nasser was a charismatic leader who used his political power against the Muslim Brotherhood.

**ANOTHER WAR** In May 1967, regional conflict flared again. Vowing to defeat the Jewish state, Nasser massed his armies on the Sinai Peninsula. Meanwhile, Syrian and Jordanian troops also mobilized for war. On June 5, 1967, the Israel Defense Forces (IDF) struck first, launching air strikes that destroyed Arab air forces before they'd left the ground. In just six days of combat, Israel captured significant territory from Egypt, Syria, and Jordan.

In Egypt and the rest of the Arab world, the Six-Day War—the

Israeli forces left Arab planes smoldering on their runways during the Six-Day War. The war was a spark for greater fundamentalism in Egypt and throughout the region.

second humiliating defeat in twenty years at the hands of Israel—brought new life to fundamentalist Islamic movements. The Muslim Brotherhood, though still outlawed, nevertheless began to recruit new members, many of whom belonged to Egypt's military and the security services. These professionals were seeking spiritual answers to the devastating national defeat. Recruits were organized into secret underground cells (subgroups) led by Sheikh Omar Abdel Rahman. Rahman, a cleric and a prominent leader in the brotherhood, called for underground activities to overthrow the government of Anwar el-Sadat, who succeeded Nasser after his death in 1970.

The group that emerged from the fiery sermons in the mosques of Cairo and Alexandria was al-Jihad—"Holy War." Also known as Egyptian Islamic Jihad, the newly formed group recruited members from all facets of Egyptian society but especially from the ranks of the armed forces and the security services. Al-Jihad's underground cells received spiritual leadership from clerics including Rahman.

## RAISING THE STAKES
President Sadat was well aware of the Islamic fundamentalists' influence inside the country, especially within the military. Seeking a victory against Israel that would both avenge 1967's loss and pacify the fundamentalists, Sadat and his

# SHEIKH OMAR ABDEL RAHMAN

Omar Abdel Rahman was born in 1938 into a poverty-stricken Egyptian family. Blinded by diabetes when he was ten months old, Rahman went on to immerse himself in Islamic studies, proving to be a brilliant religious student. By age eleven, the stories go, he had memorized a Braille copy of the Quran.

Omar Abdel Rahman

In 1967 Egypt's military defeat changed Rahman forever. Outraged by his country's humiliation by Israel, he grew more zealous, bitter, and radical in his fundamentalism. Most of his rage was directed against the nation's political leaders, or the "New Pharaohs," as they were called in Cairo's mosques.

Egyptian authorities knew that Rahman was the spiritual figure behind Islamic fundamentalist terrorist groups and that the blind preacher had a wide following. Afraid that arresting or assassinating him would only make him a more beloved cult hero, they leniently permitted him to travel throughout the Middle East, raising money and finding recruits. ■

commanders planned an attack. It would correspond with both Ramadan—one of Islam's holiest months—and with Yom Kippur, the most important Jewish holiday. On October 6, 1973, Egyptian forces crossed the Suez Canal into the Sinai Peninsula. At the same time, Syrian forces streamed into Israel from the north.

The operation was initially a success, with the Egyptian military seizing the Sinai Peninsula from the IDF. Reclaiming the Sinai Peninsula became a source of tremendous national pride. But the Yom Kippur War would not end in victory for Egypt and Syria. After eighteen days of brutal conflict, Israeli tanks were pushing on to Damascus, Syria, and Israeli forces were only one hundred miles away from Cairo.

In the wake of yet another Arab defeat and facing a national economy drained by war expenses, Sadat began to see compromise with

Israel as Egypt's best option. In what many in the Middle East considered an unthinkable move, Sadat flew from Cairo to Jerusalem in October 1977 to seek peace and reconciliation.

Sadat's journey to Jerusalem and the peace accords that he and Israeli prime minister Menachem Begin signed in 1979 were seen in many Arab capitals as a betrayal of Arab unity and of Islam. Fundamentalists vowed to punish all those responsible for a peace treaty with the Jewish state. Radical clerics in Cairo's mosques portrayed the Egyptian leader as the greatest threat to Islam since the Crusades. Then, in 1980, Rahman issued a fatwa (Islamic edict) calling for

The peace talks between Anwar el-Sadat *(left)* and Menachem Begin *(right)* angered many fundamentalists.

Sadat's assassination. His call would not go unheeded. Al-Jihad—with members inside the armed forces and with access to weapons, explosives, and detailed security information—was the group best equipped to plan and execute a history-changing operation.

■ ■ ■ ■ ■ ■ ■ ■ ■ ■ ■ ■ ■ ■ ■ ■ ■ ■ ■ ■ ■ ■ ■ ■ ■ ■ ■ ■ ■ ■ ■ ■ ■ ■

### *Death of a President*

***October 6, 1981,*** *was a grand day for a parade in Cairo. Early morning light bathed the Egyptian capital in a warm, bright glow. A pleasant breeze blew from the Nile River. For weeks crews had been cleaning the city's streets in preparation for the day's festivities, a national celebration capped by a large military parade. October 6, marking the anniversary of Egypt's 1973 capture of the Sinai Peninsula, had become one of Egypt's most important holidays.*

*That afternoon President Anwar el-Sadat, together with most of the Egyptian military's high command and members of the government, sat in the plush reviewing stand to watch the parade.*

*Representatives of Egypt's military marched by. Sadat squinted at the sunny sky as a squadron of Soviet-built MiG-23 fighter bombers, the pride of the Egyptian air force, flew overhead in a rigid formation.*

*Suddenly, soldiers riding past the stand in one of the parade's many trucks pulled out grenades and turned their machine guns toward the reviewing stand. The barrage of gunfire and the explosions that followed were furious and unforgiving. When it was over, Sadat was dead and dozens of others were wounded. Al-Jihad had struck. An opening shot had been fired in the Islamic fundamentalist revolution.*

Sadat *(top)* waves to the crowd on his way to watch a military parade in Cairo. Moments later, the Egyptian president had been shot and killed by al-Jihad terrorists.

News of Sadat's assassination spread jubilation through the mosques and slums of Egypt. Meanwhile, Egyptian authorities arrested thousands of fundamentalists on charges of involvement in the murder. Hundreds were eventually convicted and sentenced to time in Egyptian

After Sadat's assassination, many Egyptian fundamentalists were arrested and jailed. These prisoners hold up copies of the Quran.

prisons. Many more were tortured by the authorities, while others involved in the attack were banished from Egypt and prevented from entering most other Arab countries. Many of these exiled fundamentalists traveled to Afghanistan, where an army of Arab Muslims had been assembling to fight invaders from the Soviet Union. Others went to Western Europe or the United States.

Sadat's successor, Hosni Mubarak, was determined to crush the subversive Islamic movement that was challenging the Egyptian government. Al-Jihad was equally determined to change that government. The group began targeting high-level Egyptian ministers for assassination, and its attacks included the 1993 attempts on the lives of Interior Minister Hassan al-Alfi and Prime Minister Atef Sedky.

## NEW VIOLENCE

Another Egyptian Islamic terrorist group to gain force after the chaos surrounding Sadat's assassination was al-Gamaa al-Islamiya. The group had first formed in the 1970s as an extremist underground movement. Like al-Jihad, it sought the establishment of an Islamic state in Egypt. The group was split into hundreds of secret, self-contained cells with names such as Islamic Liberation Party, Excommunication and Emigration, and Saved from the Inferno. Most of al-Gamaa al-Islamiya's founders were Islamic clerics serving time in

Egyptian jails or underground leaders teaching in mosques and universities. The group's leaders, too, had felt President Sadat's peace accords with Israel to be the ultimate betrayal of Islam. They vowed revenge against the Egyptian government and promised to continue the struggle until Sharia was the law of the land.

In June 1995, al-Gamaa al-Islamiya assassins nearly succeeded in killing President Mubarak during a visit to Ethiopia. On the whole, however, the group did not focus its operations on government officials. Instead, much of al-Gamaa al-Islamiya's terrorist activity concentrated on Egyptian economic targets. Its members tended to come from the poorest sections of Egyptian society. Many joined the movement seeking an escape from economic despair and endless unemployment. As a result, the group's campaign was as much an economic struggle as it was a religious one.

President Hosni Mubarak vowed to combat al-Gamaa al-Islamiya's assault on the Egyptian government.

Hoping to inflict crippling economic damage on the government, al-Gamaa al-Islamiya looked to Egypt's vast tourism industry. The business brought millions of foreign tourists—who brought billions of dollars with them—to Egypt each year to see the pyramids, the Sphinx, and other sights. Aiming to damage the country's image in the eyes of those valuable visitors, al-Gamaa al-Islamiya terrorists made foreigners their primary targets. Tourist buses, hotels, and popular sights were bombed and machine-gunned.

■ ■ ■ ■ ■ ■ ■ ■ ■ ■ ■ ■ ■ ■ ■ ■ ■ ■ ■ ■ ■ ■ ■ ■ ■ ■ ■ ■ ■ ■ ■ ■

### *Terror in the Valley of the Kings*

**The 3,400-year-old Queen Hatshepsut Temple,** *located near Luxor in the Valley of the Kings, was a must-see for tourists to Egypt. It was also isolated, remote, and without proper communications and police coverage. Al-Gamaa al-Islamiya knew these important facts, and they planned to use them.*

*On November 17, 1997, nearly one dozen al-Gamaa al-Islamiya attackers, armed with assault rifles and machetes, massacred sixty-five tourists. Executing victims who had nowhere to run and no hope of assistance, the terrorists shot them in the head or slit their throats. Many were beheaded. Others were left with Islamic fatwas affixed to their bellies. It was one of the most brutal terrorist attacks ever perpetrated in Egypt.*

Before al-Gamaa al-Islamiya's vicious attack, the Queen Hatshepsut Temple was one of Egypt's top tourist destinations. Afterward most foreigners were too frightened to visit.

The Egyptian government responded to the Valley of the Kings attack with great force. The police, army, and intelligence services went to war against the Islamic underground, arresting thousands of al-Jihad and al-Gamaa al-Islamiya activists and their supporters. They raided mosques and killed hundreds in gun battles in the slums of Cairo and Alexandria, as well as in smaller outlying villages.

While the Egyptian government's campaign was widely criticized by international human rights groups, it was effective. Many al-Jihad and al-Gamaa al-Islamiya leaders fled the country. But they did not plan to give up their struggle against Mubarak's regime and the Westernized secular government in Cairo. Instead, they joined forces, taking up arms alongside other fundamentalist groups in the Arab world.

# DEADLY FORCE:
# LEBANON'S HEZBOLLAH

Lebanon's location at a geographical crossroads, linking Mediterranean nations with the rest of the Middle East, makes it a highly valuable area. Beginning with its earliest history under the Phoenicians, Lebanon was a major trading and economic center. Later the region was dominated by foreign rulers including the Assyrians, the Babylonians, the Persians, the Greeks, the Romans, the Ottomans, and the French.

Modern Lebanon, independent since 1943, has struggled with conflict due to internal ethnic divisions. The country is home to many ethnic and religious groups, each in competition with the others for economic and political dominance. Muslim groups include the Sunnis, the Shiites, the Druze, the Alawites, and the Ismailis, while Christian denominations include the Maronites, the Roman Catholics, the Greek Orthodox, and the Armenian Orthodox. To keep the peace, the secular Lebanese government strove to divide power proportionately among the various factions. Nevertheless, one group that suffered ongoing oppression was the Shiite Muslim sect. Shiites, forming about one-third of the population, were the largest ethnic and

Lebanon has often found itself embroiled in conflicts among its neighbors.

religious group inside the country, but they were the poorest as well. With little political voice and often at the mercy of the more influential Maronite Christians and Sunni Muslims, the Shiites were powerless in a nation in which they were the majority.

## CHANGES AND CHALLENGES

After the 1948 Arab-Israeli War, a new threat to Lebanon's ethnic and religious balance arose, as thousands of Palestinian refugees streamed into the country. They crowded into camps outside Lebanon's capital of Beirut, near the Lebanese-Israeli border, and along the Mediterranean coast. Then, in 1970, legions of Palestinian fighters who had been expelled from Israeli-held areas arrived in Lebanon, intending to use the country as an international base of operations for terrorist attacks against Israeli targets.

The influx threatened Lebanon's already delicate peace. Many Lebanese, especially Christian residents, opposed the presence of the Palestinians. In addition, Lebanese-based Palestinian terrorist attacks on Israel sparked swift and fierce Israeli retaliation. With tensions at a fever pitch among the many factions, Lebanon erupted into civil war in 1975.

In March 1978, Israel invaded southern Lebanon in response to a Palestinian attack. To prevent the Palestinians from regrouping after the Israeli withdrawal a few months later, Israel helped to establish a

Beginning in the 1970s, civil war tore Lebanon apart.

Christian-led South Lebanon Army (SLA). That same month, yet another new military element entered the scene. Iran's shah (ruler) sent a group of soldiers to participate in a UN peacekeeping mission whose goal was to separate Israeli and Palestinian forces in southern Lebanon. The Iranian troopers, nearly seven hundred in all, were devoutly religious followers of the Shiite cleric Ayatollah Ruhollah Khomeini. When an Islamic revolution toppled Iran's shah one year later, Khomeini became the country's spiritual and political leader. Spreading the Islamic revolution to other nations became a top national priority. The Iranian peacekeepers in Lebanon soon took on the role of encouraging Shiites to create their own Islamic revolution.

Tired of poverty and powerlessness, thousands of Lebanese Shiites flocked to Beirut mosques, where they listened to fiery sermons urging them to take up arms against their Westernized, non-Islamic government. The Ayatollah Khomeini's government supported the Shiite effort in Lebanon with weapons, funds, and terrorist training. The Iranians also helped organize a range of religious groups and youth clubs into a single political party seeking to establish a Shiite state in Lebanon.

## HEZBOLLAH EMERGES
Meanwhile, Lebanon's civil war raged. Following another Israeli invasion in June 1982, Palestinian terrorists were expelled from Lebanon as part of a cease-fire agreement. Lebanese Shiites hoped to fill a power vacuum left by the retreating Palestinians, but they faced challenges from Israeli forces and from groups including the SLA. Then, in September 1982, Christian militias entered Lebanon's Sabra and Shatila refugee camps.

The Israeli invasion of Lebanon in 1982 created still greater friction within the region.

# IRAN'S ISLAMIC REVOLUTION

Heir to the great Persian Empire and situated atop vast oil reserves, Iran was once a major Middle Eastern power. But in the 1970s, it was torn by turmoil. The authority of its ruler, Reza Shah Pahlavi, had been reinforced by massive American military support. Many Iranians, especially the poor and the politically oppressed, despised the shah's pro-Western policies. But they were unable to express their political voice or to challenge the shah's secret police.

Economic difficulties added to Iran's troubles. By the late 1970s, government corruption and the shah's failure to share the nation's oil wealth with the masses sparked widespread discontent. The presence of thousands of European and American workers in the country was also seen by many Iranians as evidence that their misery was due to Western influences.

Many Iranians turned to the mosques and the messages of fundamentalist clerics. The most revered of these clerics was the Shiite leader Ayatollah Ruhollah Khomeini. Exiled to Iraq and later to France for his antigovernment preaching, Khomeini became a cult hero whose sermons condemning the shah and urging revolution were taped and smuggled into Iran.

As discontent mounted, many Iranians took to the streets in protest. Demonstrators throughout the country demanded the shah's removal and the establishment of an Islamic state led by the Ayatollah. In September 1978, the gatherings

The Ayatollah Khomeini greets his followers.

turned violent. The shah declared martial law, and bloody clashes followed. Finally, on January 16, 1979, the shah left the country, supposedly on a short holiday. He never returned. Shortly thereafter, Khomeini returned, portraying himself as a savior who would restore Islamic pride and morals in Iran. Still vehemently anti-American and anti-Western, Iran went on to support Islamic fundamentalist terrorism throughout the Middle East. ■

The militias carried out a massacre of Palestinian civilians in the camps, in revenge for a Christian leader's assassination. Peacekeepers from the United States, France, and Italy arrived to help stabilize the country.

The presence of the foreign troops was a final spur to the Shiite movement, which had been steadily gaining support. Iran took advantage of the turmoil, sending fighters from its Revolutionary Guard to help set up a more forceful and organized revolutionary Islamic movement. Syria, with a strongly anti-Israel stance, also supported the new organization, which became known as Hezbollah—the Arabic word for "Party of God."

Sheikh Mohammed Hussein Fadlallah

The spiritual father of the Lebanese movement was Sheikh Mohammed Hussein Fadlallah, a prominent leader of Lebanon's Shiite community. Based in the area of Baalbek in northern Lebanon's Bekáa Valley, Hezbollah was soon able to gain a foothold in the slums of West Beirut. Young and highly capable Shiites flocked to Hezbollah recruitment centers to form the organization's military and terrorist base.

Financially and militarily supported by Iran and Syria, Hezbollah committed itself to waging a terrorist war against Israel. Israel still controlled a large portion of Lebanon. According to Hezbollah leaders, Israeli agents were carrying out a brutal campaign of hostage taking, imprisonment, and even murder against Lebanese Muslims—especially Shiites. One of Hezbollah's goals was the release of Lebanese Shiites in Israeli jails. At the same time, Hezbollah targeted U.S. peacekeeping troops.

## NEW TACTICS

Many Hezbollah members had watched the Palestinians fight for years, without success, for an independent state. Determined that their own mission to establish a Shiite Lebanon would fare better, the organization's commanders rewrote the rules of warfare.

# HEZBOLLAH'S OPERATIONAL RULES

According to documents seized in Lebanon, Hezbollah's combat doctrine is designed to wear down an enemy in a bloody and prolonged war.

1. Keep away from superior force. Always attack the weak and then prepare to disengage quickly.
2. Protecting the lives of our own warriors is more important than taking the lives of our enemy.
3. Attack only when success is assured.
4. Absolute surprise is essential. If you have been discovered, you have failed.
5. Do not get bogged down in a conventional battle where the enemy's strength can be used to our disadvantage.
6. Executing a mission and hitting a target requires patience and perseverance.
7. Attack means movement and movement forward.
8. Keep your enemy in fear—on the front lines and in the rear.
9. The path to total victory is paved by achieving thousands of smaller victories.
10. Keep your fighters motivated and dedicated to final victory.
11. The media is worth an infinite number of artillery cannons. Use them to your advantage.
12. The indigenous population is an invaluable resource—look after it.
13. Hurt the enemy slowly, then cripple and kill him. ■

Hezbollah members

Imad Mughniyah, commander of Hezbollah's special terrorist operations arm, the Special Security Apparatus, would unleash a force to send the Middle East reeling: suicide bombers.

■ ■ ■ ■ ■ ■ ■ ■ ■ ■ ■ ■ ■ ■ ■ ■ ■ ■ ■ ■ ■ ■ ■ ■ ■ ■ ■ ■ ■ ■ ■

## *Under Fire*

**The rage that festered** *in the Shiite slums of West Beirut was powerful. It found its strength in the desire to right the historical wrong done to Lebanon's Shiites and in a hatred for U.S. interference in Lebanese matters. Hezbollah began a bombing campaign that would stun the United States.*

*The onslaught began on April 18, 1983, when a Hezbollah operative drove a truck crammed with explosives through the front gate of the U.S. embassy in Beirut. The blast devastated the building and killed sixty-three people, seventeen of them Americans.*

*Hezbollah's next attack would be even more horrific. On October 23, 1983, Hezbollah suicide bombers struck the U.S. Marine barracks at the southern entrance to Beirut International Airport. The explosion, so large that it registered as an earth tremor, decimated the flimsy sleeping quarters, killing 241 U.S. servicepeople and wounding*

Hezbollah's bombing of the U.S. embassy in Beirut left the building in shambles and scores of people dead.

*more than 100 others. That same day, a Hezbollah suicide bomber drove another truck full of explosives through the barracks of the French peacekeeping contingent in West Beirut, killing 58 paratroopers. Then, on December 12, 1983, Hezbollah terrorists drove a truck packed with explosives through the front gates of the U.S. embassy in Kuwait City, Kuwait, killing six.*

*The United States had no military response for Hezbollah's assault. Hidden deep within the slums of West Beirut and in the Bekáa Valley, Hezbollah was a difficult foe to find and defeat. For the United States—a superpower experienced only in large-scale conventional wars—an underground enemy willing to die in battle meant a new kind of war.*

■ ■ ■ ■ ■ ■ ■ ■ ■ ■ ■ ■ ■ ■ ■ ■ ■ ■ ■ ■ ■ ■ ■ ■ ■ ■ ■ ■ ■

U.S. leaders feared that retaliation for the attacks might plunge the region—which was enjoying a shaky peace following a Lebanese-Israeli treaty that had been signed in May—into renewed war. But inaction led only to new attacks and a new tactic: kidnapping. Between 1983 and 1985, Hezbollah squads kidnapped more than one dozen French and American citizens working and living in Beirut. The hostages included clerics, academics, and reporters who were interrogated and tortured. Some were savagely beaten by Imad Mughniyah himself. Two of the most notable abductions were those of the American reporter Terry Anderson, who was held for seven years before his release, and of Central Intelligence Agency (CIA) station chief William Buckley. Seized outside his West Beirut apartment, Buckley would die in captivity.

■ ■ ■ ■ ■ ■ ■ ■ ■ ■ ■ ■ ■ ■ ■ ■ ■ ■ ■ ■ ■ ■ ■ ■ ■ ■ ■ ■ ■

*Attack in the Skies*

**Hezbollah terrorists** *had proven their fearlessness in suicide bombings and kidnappings. But still outraged at the holding of Lebanese Shiites in Israeli prisons, the group's commanders wanted more. Soon they would also show their skills at air piracy.*

*On June 14, 1985, TWA Flight 847 was scheduled to fly from Athens, Greece, to Rome, Italy. Among the passengers boarding the Boeing jet were two young Arab men who had hidden guns and grenades in their bags. Less than half an hour into the flight, the* gunmen brandished their weapons and forced the pilot to divert the flight to Beirut. News cameras caught footage of the terrified pilot leaning out of the cockpit at gunpoint, as the terrorists warned officials to comply with their wishes.

Demanding the release of seven hundred Shiite prisoners held in Israel, the hijackers released some of the women and children on the plane and demanded that the jet be refueled. They then kept the plane bouncing restlessly between Beirut and Algiers, Algeria, landing to refuel, to release more hostages, to reiterate their demands, and to bring more terrorists, weapons, and supplies onto the plane. During one of their stops in Beirut, the gunmen tortured and murdered Robert Dean Stethem, a young officer in the U.S. Navy. They dumped his body onto the Beirut airport's tarmac.

A Hezbollah member waves a gun out the cockpit window of hijacked TWA Flight 847. The plane's captain, John Testrake, is visible behind the terrorist.

The remaining hostages were held for seventeen days, until Israel, under intense political pressure from the U.S. government, agreed to release some of its Shiite prisoners. The Hezbollah hijackers released the remaining hostages and fled into the Shiite neighborhoods of Beirut. The United States took no military action but placed several of the hijackers on the Federal Bureau of Investigation's (FBI's) Most Wanted List, vowing to track them down and bring them to justice.

Meanwhile, the suicide bombings continued. On March 17, 1992, in one of Hezbollah's farthest-reaching operations, a truck bombing obliterated the Israeli embassy in Buenos Aires, Argentina, killing twenty-nine and wounding some one hundred. In July 1994, a truck laden with nearly one ton of explosives exploded outside the Argentine-Israeli Mutual Association community center in Buenos Aires. Eighty-six were killed in that blast and hundreds more were critically wounded.

Rescue and security workers stand atop the rubble of the Israeli embassy in Buenos Aires after a Hezbollah attack.

In all, over a period of about sixteen years, Hezbollah suicide bombers and commando squads killed more than two thousand Israelis. This devastating death toll eventually led the Israeli government to withdraw its forces from Lebanon in 2000. This success against Israel was deeply admired by many Palestinians militants, and Hezbollah has come to play an important part in the Palestinian conflict with Israel.

At the same time, the group has also taken on a more active political role. With its own television station, about one dozen representatives in Lebanon's parliament, and a far-reaching network of schools, hospitals, and other social programs, the Party of God has considerable influence. It is poised to do whatever is necessary to give Lebanese Shiites an ever greater voice in their country's future.

# UNCHECKED WRATH:
# ALGERIA'S GROUPE ISLAMIQUE ARMÉ

Algeria, a nation of more than 31 million inhabitants, has long been a land in turmoil. Located in North Africa on the coast of the Mediterranean Sea, Algeria spent more than one century under French control. In the twentieth century, dissatisfaction with French rule—and particularly with French repression of Algeria's Muslim majority—fed growing nationalism and Islamic fundamentalist movements. Tensions mounted steadily for years, finally erupting into a war of independence in 1954.

Algerian rebels fighting for independence were led politically by the Front de Libération Nationale (National Liberation Front, or FLN) and militarily by the Armée de Libération Nationale (National Liberation Army, or ALN). They launched terrorist attacks against French military and government targets in Algeria. The FLN and ALN later

Algeria's history and troubles are tightly bound to France.

Algerian rebels train for battle during the nation's war of independence against France.

expanded their targets to include civilians. French forces responded to the strikes with equal force, and the war dragged on for eight years.

| **POLITICAL TIDES** | Algeria finally won its independence from France in 1962. Independence brought its own challenges, however. The war had left the country with a shattered economy and infrastructure. Residents endured enormous unemployment and crushing poverty. In addition, struggles for power soon broke out, some of them escalating into armed clashes in the country's provinces.

Amid such turbulence, the independent nation's first president, Ahmed Ben Bella, was ousted after only two years in office. His defense minister, Colonel Houari Boumédienne, took over and pledged to modernize the nation's economy and industry. To fund the transformation, Boumédienne tapped into Algeria's enormous oil reserves, estimated to be worth more than $60 billion. However, even with oil production up, the nation still faced enormous difficulties. Algerian farms struggled to produce enough food for the country's people. With an increasing birthrate and the migration of large numbers of rural Algerians to Algiers and other cities, poverty and crime levels rose. Discontent rose too.

President Houari Boumédienne

By the time Colonel Chadli Benjedid succeeded Boumédienne in 1978, the nation depended heavily on oil. When world oil prices collapsed in the mid-1980s, Algeria experienced a full-fledged economic disaster. Unemployment, hunger, and poverty skyrocketed. Anger at the government—which many people believed was corrupt and which was still strongly guided and funded by France—festered in the slums of Algiers. In addition, Francophiles—a small percentage of the country's population who identified with their French roots and who controlled much of the nation's wealth—were increasingly despised. Their non-Islamic habits and their influence in the country were especially frowned upon and resented. Strikes and riots became commonplace. Then, in October 1988, a large street demonstration spiraled into violence. The government declared a state of national emergency, and the Algerian army was called out to suppress the riots. The government forces killed an estimated five hundred protesters and arrested several thousand more.

The army's harsh response to what was later called "Black October" sparked even greater rage throughout Algeria. Benjedid scrambled to hold his government together, but it proved to be a losing battle. By 1989 the newly formed Front Islamique du Salut (Islamic Salvation Front, or FIS) had emerged as the country's dominant opposition movement to Benjedid's government. The FIS was primarily a moderate Islamic party. By setting up facilities such as food banks, job training, and medical clinics to provide basic services to the country's poor, the party had built a broad base of support. In June 1990, the FIS won by a landslide in local elections.

Those in power in Algeria—and in France—were reluctant to let an Islamic party take control of the country. The central Algerian government soon introduced election laws intended to prevent the FIS from winning future campaigns. In 1991, however, in a series of national elections, the FIS again gained enormous political power. As the second round of elections approached, the military decided to cancel the elections to prevent an FIS victory. Algerian Muslims were outraged. The situation deteriorated further in January 1992, when President Benjedid resigned under intense pressure from his advisers and military commanders. The army promptly took over the day-to-day affairs of the country, banning the FIS and all public gatherings. Heavily armed police officers patrolled street corners in the capital. Thousands of FIS members were arrested, tortured, and imprisoned.

FIS members gather in Algiers to protest against the government's suppression of elections.

## A NEW FORCE

Out of Algeria's unrest emerged the Groupe Islamique Armé (Armed Islamic Group, or GIA). A fundamentalist Islamic terrorist group, the GIA was determined to bring the FIS to power and to place a strong Islamic government in control of Algeria. To achieve these goals, the GIA's leaders planned to use terrorism to make the secular government unable to function or maintain control over the country.

GIA operatives began a campaign of horrific attacks against politicians, judges, journalists, and civilians. In August 1992, GIA members bombed the international airport in Algiers, killing nine people and injuring dozens. In 1993 the group declared that all foreigners must leave the country or face their own deaths. In subsequent years, GIA operatives kidnapped dozens of foreign workers and diplomats, usually executing them by slitting their throats or shooting them. In addition, GIA leaders advocated the kidnapping and murder of Christian nuns, priests, and other non-Islamic religious workers, while also vowing to punish Muslims whom they did not see as being strict enough in their observance of Islam.

Like other fundamentalist Islamic organizations seeking the establishment of Islamic states, the GIA views the United States and Israel as traditional enemies. However, the GIA has also carried out many operations against French targets, seeing France's colonization and rule of Algeria as one of the factors resulting in the nation's secular, Westernized government. In addition, a large population of Algerian emigrants lives in France's biggest cities, making the nation an obvious European base of operations for the GIA.

# THE CALL TO ARMS

In a nation torn by poverty and war, the radical justice proposed by the GIA appealed to many young Algerian men. Without work and without hope, they flocked to GIA recruiters to join the fight. As they saw it, the moderate stance of the FIS had only led to defeat. Only a strong fundamentalist approach could create a free, Islamic Algeria.

Divided into many cells of a few dozen operatives each, the GIA is believed to have many leaders at different levels of the operation, rather than one central figure. Many GIA operatives also came from Afghanistan as veterans of the Islamic army that fought against Soviet invaders of that nation in the 1980s. Many of these fighters, in turn, had gone to Afghanistan from Egypt, the cradle of Islamic fundamentalism. ■

After the cancellation of the 1992 elections, the unrest in Algeria spiraled into chaos. As the GIA grew more active, the government responded by placing heavily armed guards in Algiers and throughout the country.

■ ■ ■ ■ ■ ■ ■ ■ ■ ■ ■ ■ ■ ■ ■ ■ ■ ■ ■ ■ ■ ■ ■ ■ ■ ■ ■ ■ ■ ■ ■

*Flight of Fear*

***December 24, 1994.*** *Air France Flight 8969 was headed from Algiers to Paris that Christmas Eve day with more than two hundred passengers. But the French travelers on board would not be home in time for the holidays. Before the airliner could take off from Houari Boumédienne Airport, four GIA operatives dressed as airline officials pulled out guns and hand grenades. Shooting one passenger dead, they announced that the plane was being hijacked.*

*For thirty-six hours, the plane remained on the tarmac in Algiers. Although the terrorists released about fifty women, children, and elderly passengers, they killed two more hostages before finally ordering the pilot to fly across the Mediterranean to Marseille, France. Once on the ground in France, the terrorists demanded that the aircraft's tanks be filled with twenty-seven tons of explosive jet fuel. They would then be ready to carry out their plan—to crash their airborne bomb, full of hostages and fuel, into the Eiffel Tower in Paris.*

*The French, however, were not about to allow the hijacked jet to take off again once it was on the ground in Marseille. Fifty-four hours after the terror had begun, French counterterrorist commandos*

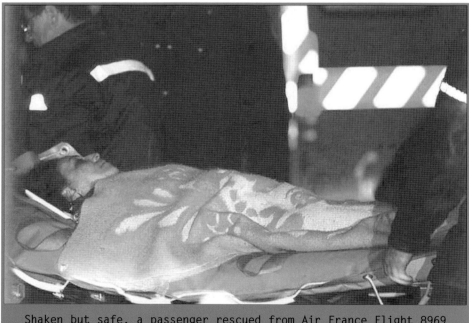

Shaken but safe, a passenger rescued from Air France Flight 8969 is carried away on a stretcher.

*stormed the plane. Tossing stun grenades that filled the cabin with smoke and confusion, they rushed into the cockpit. Within five minutes, all four of the GIA terrorists were dead. The 177 passengers left on board had been saved.*

■ ■ ■ ■ ■ ■ ■ ■ ■ ■ ■ ■ ■ ■ ■ ■ ■ ■ ■ ■ ■ ■ ■ ■ ■ ■ ■ ■ ■ ■ ■

Although the Air France hijacking had failed, the GIA continued to strike against French targets, bombing the Paris subway and other sites in France. Within Algeria itself, terrorist attacks carried out by the GIA and other armed opposition factions, including a military offshoot of the FIS called the Islamic Salvation Army (AIS), plunged the nation into the equivalent of a civil war.

Throughout the 1990s, the GIA employed widespread assassinations and bombings, many of them taking place in the hinterland south of Algiers. Algerian civilians were increasingly targeted in this violent conflict. Armed militants slaughtered whole villages in bloody raids, leaving dozens and sometimes hundreds dead. The attackers were brutal, often beheading their victims or slitting their throats. Although the government denies ever having any involvement in these acts, many Algerians believe that some of the civilian massacres were actually carried out by the government's security services who then

Village massacres, each leaving dozens dead, terrorized the Algerian countryside throughout the 1990s. The bodies of these victims are wrapped in Algerian flags.

blamed the murders on Islamic militants. In all, it is estimated that more than 100,000 people were killed in less than one decade of conflict.

In 1997 the AIS signed a cease-fire with the Algerian government. Since then the level of fighting in Algeria has dropped. In about 1998, the GIA's role as the most prominent and active Algerian terrorist group was taken over by one of its splinter groups, the Salafist Group for Preaching and Combat (GSPC).

These members of the Salafist Group for Preaching and Combat were arrested in Europe on suspicion of plotting terrorist activities.

Nevertheless, GIA members remain committed to their struggle and are determined to continue the violence until an Islamic government is in place. Still claiming hundreds or perhaps thousands of supporters and guerrillas operating in Algeria and in underground cells in Europe, the GIA remains a formidable terrorist force.

# GLOBAL TERROR:
## AL-QAEDA'S
# INTERNATIONAL NETWORK

For years most Islamic terrorist movements focused on achieving specific local goals. The idea of an international movement—an alliance bringing together many different groups, languages, and cultures bound together by Islamic fundamentalism—represented a powerful change.

| THE IDEA TAKES SHAPE | One of the first supporters of an international Islamic movement was the Palestinian cleric Abdullah Yusuf Azzam. Born in British-held Palestine in 1941, Azzam became a refugee after Israel's creation. As an adult, he traveled to mosques throughout the Middle East, delivering spellbinding sermons. Azzam urged the Islamic world to free itself from injustice and oppression and to rise up in a unified assault against Israel.

After the Arab loss in the 1967 war, Azzam joined the Muslim Brotherhood and made contacts in Egypt, eventually attending college in Cairo. In the mid-1970s, he traveled to Saudi Arabia to teach at a university. But Azzam's academic career was cut short by the Soviet invasion of Afghanistan in December 1979. The Soviet Union—a Communist

Abdullah Yusuf Azzam envisioned a transnational fundamentalist network.

superpower—sent thousands of troops into Afghanistan, claiming that its goal was to support Afghanistan's struggling Communist government. However, many Muslims saw the invasion as an epic struggle between the Soviet Union, whose government was strongly secular, and a much smaller Muslim neighbor. Fiery calls were raised for an Islamic revolution.

Heeding that call, Azzam traveled to northwestern Pakistan, near the Afghan border. As Muslim volunteers arrived from around the region, Azzam organized them into a band of resistance fighters. With Azzam as a leader, the fighters, who were called mujahideen, prepared to wage a jihad against the Soviets. Within Afghanistan's native population, rebel fighters followed various leaders, including Ahmad Shah Massoud, a member of his country's educated minority.

The revered mujahideen leader Ahmad Shah Massoud *(above right)* commanded many of Afghanistan's rebels, while Azzam helped to recruit and organize more fighters.

**BIN LADEN AND AL-QAEDA** | One of Azzam's most valuable volunteers was a young millionaire from Saudi Arabia named Osama bin Laden. This dedicated recruit would provide the mujahideen with seemingly endless streams of money.

Osama bin Laden was born in 1957, the son of one of Saudi Arabia's most prominent families. Bin Laden's father owned a construction company favored by the Saudi king and was one of the kingdom's richest men.

Osama bin Laden, however, cared little about the family business. He had enjoyed his wealth as a youth, buying flashy cars and attending parties. But while in college in Cairo, he discovered the world of Islamic fundamentalism and came to share Azzam's vision of a global struggle against the West. Shortly after the Soviet invasion, bin Laden traveled to Pakistan and Afghanistan to do his part for the jihad.

Osama bin Laden, shown on the Arabic television station al-Jazeera, was skilled at spreading the message of jihad to Muslims throughout the Middle East.

Bin Laden spent the first few years of the Afghan-Soviet War raising cash for the fight against the Soviets. Through his family's company, he moved trucks and other construction tools into Afghanistan, using them to build roads and burrows for the mujahideen. As the conflict intensified, he sought a more active role. Wearing military jackets over his traditional Arab robes and carrying a captured Soviet rifle, he joined the fighting on the front.

Azzam and bin Laden were natural allies, and they established a recruiting center called Maktab al-Khidamat (MAK). MAK offices were set up all over the world, encouraging young Muslims to fight in Afghanistan. Bin Laden helped pay for the transportation of new recruits to Afghanistan. He also funded the setup of sophisticated training facilities, where expert instructors tutored recruits in guerrilla warfare, sabotage, and undercover operations.

With bin Laden's cash and Azzam's zeal, the international Muslim army being assembled in Pakistan and Afghanistan soon grew to be twenty thousand strong. It included volunteers from Libya, Tunisia, Algeria, Somalia, Ethiopia, Saudi Arabia, Jordan, Lebanon, Syria, Iraq, Turkey, Indonesia, the Philippines, and many other nations. At the same time, the mujahideen received arms and funding from the United States, which was in the middle of the long Cold War with the Soviet Union. Although these hostilities never erupted into actual war, the two nations competed militarily, scientifically, and politically with one another. By aiding the Afghan mujahideen in their struggle against the invasion, the U.S. government hoped to combat growing Soviet power.

In 1989 Azzam was killed in a surprise bombing. Some observers believed that bin Laden had arranged the assassination, hoping to gain more power for himself. Whatever the case, bin Laden carried on the struggle. After the Soviet withdrawal from Afghanistan that same year, bin Laden created a new organization called al-Qaeda, or "the Base," to continue the jihad and to take it beyond Afghanistan.

Bin Laden envisioned al-Qaeda as a hub for international Islamic fundamentalism, and he planned to run terrorist training camps in Afghanistan and Pakistan to prepare al-Qaeda operatives for war. However, not all mujahideen veterans joined bin Laden in his fight. Many, including Ahmad Shah Massoud, stayed in Afghanistan to help rebuild the shattered country.

## EMERGING THREAT | On August 2, 1990, Iraq invaded its

tiny neighbor Kuwait. Among the nations to respond to the aggressive Iraqi invasion was the United States. Hundreds of thousands of U.S. soldiers arrived at bases in Saudi Arabia. Stationed there, they prepared to enter Kuwait and drive out the Iraqis. Many Kuwaitis welcomed the aid of the U.S. forces.

To bin Laden, however, the presence of Western troops in Saudi Arabia—home to the holy cities of Mecca and Medina—seemed like the ultimate insult to Islam. The war became a turning point in his view of al-Qaeda's mission. He vowed vengeance against the United States.

The presence of U.S. troops on Saudi soil enraged bin Laden and fueled his fury against the West.

In the early 1990s, bin Laden's Saudi citizenship was revoked after he called on his supporters to rise against the nation's monarchy, which he viewed as corrupt. Leaving Saudi Arabia, bin Laden and a large band of his followers moved to Khartoum, Sudan. Sudan's leadership was made up of fundamentalist Muslims who allowed bin Laden's group to use the North African nation as a base. From his new headquarters, bin Laden distributed taped sermons calling for a holy war against the United States and other non-Islamic nations.

As al-Qaeda continued to take shape, it assembled an army of part-time operatives who lived around the world and were ready to be summoned to action at any time. One of the most prominent members was Sheikh Omar Abdel Rahman, who had moved to the United States and was preaching the word of the jihad to devoted followers at the al-Salaam Mosque in Jersey City, New Jersey.

But bin Laden and his mujahideen veterans remained virtually unknown to U.S. and international intelligence agencies, even after al-Qaeda directed a strike against a U.S. target. On December 29, 1992, the group bombed a hotel in Aden, Yemen, that was a rest stop for U.S. servicepeople. However, investigators could draw no direct connection between the perpetrators and bin Laden. They had no idea that bin Laden's group was already at work in New York City, laying the foundation for a surprise terrorist attack.

# THE LIEUTENANTS:
# THE MEN BEHIND OSAMA BIN LADEN

DR. AYMAN AL-ZAWAHIRI is bin Laden's top deputy and chief planner. One of al-Jihad's founding members, al-Zawahiri later traveled to Afghanistan, where he became a close associate of bin Laden. Seen with bin Laden on videotapes before and after the September 11 attacks, al-Zawahiri is believed to be in hiding.

Bin Laden *(center)* carried out his global campaign with the help of powerful aides such as al-Zawahiri *(left)* and Atef *(right).*

MOHAMMED ATEF was al-Qaeda's military commander. A former operations chief in al-Jihad, Atef played an instrumental role in Sadat's assassination. He became al-Qaeda's military commander in 1991 and is believed to have helped plan the September 11 attacks. Atef was reportedly killed by U.S. air strikes in Afghanistan in November 2001.

ABU ZUBAYDAH was al-Qaeda's operations chief. He was once al-Qaeda's chief recruiter and is believed to have recruited the nineteen September 11 hijackers. U.S. and Pakistani officers captured Zubaydah in Pakistan in March 2002.

SAIF AL-ADEL, also known as Muhamad Ibrahim Makkawi, is al-Qaeda's security chief. A former officer in the Egyptian army, al-Adel joined bin Laden in Afghanistan in the early 1980s. Al-Adel is responsible for training operatives in special operations and is believed to have personally trained some of the September 11 hijackers.

RAMZI BINALSHIBH was a key coordinator for al-Qaeda, connecting international cells of operatives. Binalshibh is believed to have helped coordinate many facets of the September 11 attacks. U.S. authorities in Pakistan captured him in September 2002. ∎

## Direct Strike

**The group**—*a motley crew of Sheikh Rahman's followers—met to review the plan one last time. They had come to the United States from Egypt, Jordan, and other nations of the Middle East. Some of them had fought in Afghanistan. All were committed to the jihad. Their mission was to assist al-Qaeda lieutenant Ramzi Yousef in a bold terrorist attack on the twin towers of New York City's World Trade Center (WTC).*

*On February 26, 1993, Yousef and his accomplices drove a rented van to a basement garage underneath the WTC's Vista Hotel. One of them carefully lit the long fuse timer. The timer would give them thirty minutes—enough time to escape across the Hudson River to New Jersey.*

*At 12:18 P.M., more than two tons of homemade explosives ripped through the depths of the parking garage. Six people were killed in the blast, and more than one thousand were wounded. The building was badly damaged. The towers, however, still stood.*

FBI agents view the destruction following al-Qaeda's 1993 bombing of the World Trade Center.

U.S. law enforcement officials swiftly caught and arrested most of the bombing's conspirators. Yousef himself, however, was gone. A few weeks earlier, he had used falsified documents to get a new passport and had purchased a one-way ticket to Pakistan. He used the ticket on the day of the bombing. And although investigators were able to tie the bombers to Sheikh Rahman, a connection to bin Laden had still not been established.

Yousef's next major assignment was "Project Bojinka," or "Project Big Bang." In one lethal twelve-hour period, Yousef and a Philippines-based al-Qaeda cell under his command planned to place homemade, undetectable bombs on eleven U.S. jets flying across the Pacific. One of the targeted aircraft was to be hijacked and crashed into CIA Headquarters in Langley, Virginia. Bojinka operatives also planned to assassinate President Bill Clinton and Pope John Paul II during trips to the Philippines.

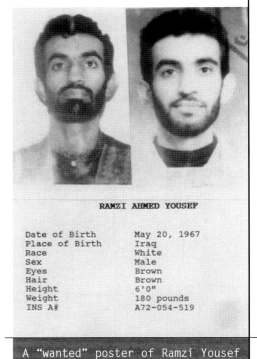

RAMZI AHMED YOUSEF

| | |
|---|---|
| Date of Birth | May 20, 1967 |
| Place of Birth | Iraq |
| Race | White |
| Sex | Male |
| Eyes | Brown |
| Hair | Brown |
| Height | 6'0" |
| Weight | 180 pounds |
| INS A# | A72-054-519 |

A "wanted" poster of Ramzi Yousef

But in January 1995, Yousef's bomb workshop caught fire. He fled, leaving behind valuable evidence of al-Qaeda's plans—evidence that finally clarified the connection between bin Laden's group and recent attacks. Yousef was captured on February 7, 1995, in Islamabad, Pakistan, by U.S. and Pakistani agents. He was flown to the United States, where he stood trial for both the World Trade Center bombing and Project Bojinka. He was convicted and sentenced to a life sentence, plus 240 years, in solitary confinement.

Nevertheless, the mid-1990s were active years for bin Laden and al-Qaeda. Still operating primarily from Sudan, the organization targeted Egypt for its repression of Egypt's fundamentalist movements and for its friendly relations with Israel. The group was believed to be responsible for the May 1995 car bombing of the Egyptian embassy in Pakistan, killing more than twenty people, and for the attempted assassination of Egyptian president Hosni Mubarak in June 1995. Bin Laden and al-Qaeda were also believed to be responsible for attacks on U.S. targets, including two

The June 1996 bombing of a U.S. military barracks *(above)* in Dhahran, Saudi Arabia, killed nineteen Americans.

bombings of U.S. military barracks in Saudi Arabia in 1995 and 1996. Even before these bombings, which received wide coverage and condemnation, international pressure on Sudan to oust bin Laden had been growing. In late 1996, bin Laden, his family, and the entire al-Qaeda organization headed to Afghanistan.

## RETURN TO AFGHANISTAN

When bin Laden arrived, Afghanistan was ruled by an extremist Islamic faction called the Taliban. Headed by a fundamentalist cleric named Mullah Mohammed Omar, the Taliban sought to establish a rigid Islamic government and society that was guided by an extremely strict interpretation of Sharia. Mullah Omar and the Taliban welcomed bin Laden and supported al-Qaeda's mission of a jihad against the West. Afghanistan soon became the new al-Qaeda headquarters.

Bin Laden's fortune, his charisma, and his reputation as a warrior of the Afghan war helped to create a larger-than-life image, which in turn drew an ever greater following. Devout Muslims from around the world, seeking answers and an escape from poverty and oppression, joined bin Laden's group. In February 1998, bin Laden announced the formation of an umbrella organization called the World Islamic Front for Jihad against Jews and Crusaders. The group brought together many fundamentalist terrorist groups, whose commanders were capable, innovative, and dedicated. Through the World Islamic Front, those groups would gain access to al-Qaeda funds and support. This support allowed the fundamentalist front to broaden and coordinate its attacks on the United States and its allies.

■ ■ ■ ■ ■ ■ ■ ■ ■ ■ ■ ■ ■ ■ ■ ■ ■ ■ ■ ■ ■ ■ ■ ■ ■ ■ ■ ■ ■ ■ ■

### *African Embassies under Attack*

*On the morning of Friday, August 7, 1998—the seventh anniversary of the arrival of U.S. troops in Saudi Arabia to fight the Iraqis—business was going on as usual at the U.S. embassy in Nairobi, Kenya. Then, at 10:38 A.M., a suicide bomber crashed a truck carrying more than one ton of explosives through the rear of the building. The blast that ripped through the embassy overturned desks, collapsed ceilings, and maimed bodies. When the smoke began to clear, 224 people were dead, and more than 5,000 had been wounded, most of them native Kenyans.*

*That same morning, in the Tanzanian capital of Dar es Salaam several hundred miles to the south, a second suicide bomber detonated a truck full of more than one ton of explosives at the outer gate of the U.S. embassy in that city. The explosion created a massive fireball and caused significant damage to the embassy. Twelve people were killed in the suicide bombing, and another eighty-five were critically wounded.*

Rescuers help survivors of the embassy bombing in Kenya out of the demolished structure.

U.S. authorities arrested several al-Qaeda agents in Kenya and Pakistan in connection with the embassy attacks, and the U.S. military also responded to al-Qaeda's threat. On August 20, 1998, U.S. Navy warships launched cruise missiles at al-Qaeda targets in Afghanistan and Sudan. The targets in Afghanistan were believed to be al-Qaeda training camps. The Sudanese target was the El Shifa Pharmaceutical Industries Company, a bin Laden-owned factory that was believed to have manufactured chemical weapons.

Meanwhile, concern mounted that al-Qaeda might be planning attacks against U.S. and Israeli targets to coincide with the new millennium. Al-Qaeda was indeed plotting to blow up Los Angeles International Airport, along with a series of hotels and sites in Jordan where American tourists would be gathered. However, greatly heightened security convinced bin Laden to wait for a time when defenses were down and a strike was least expected.

Just such an unexpected attack took place on October 12, 2000. The U.S. Navy destroyer USS *Cole* had docked in Aden, Yemen, to refuel. Suddenly, two al-Qaeda operatives rammed a skiff into the ship, detonating a blast that tore a gaping hole in the *Cole*'s side. Seventeen sailors were killed, and scores more were critically wounded.

The *Cole* bombing was a typical al-Qaeda operation. Bin Laden's strategists had selected a poorly defended target that was vulnerable to attack. That tactic would be used again on September 11, 2001.

■ ■ ■ ■ ■ ■ ■ ■ ■ ■ ■ ■ ■ ■ ■ ■ ■ ■ ■ ■ ■ ■ ■ ■ ■ ■ ■ ■ ■ ■ ■ ■ ■ ■ ■ ■

## 9/11

**September 11 began** *as a brilliantly sunny day in New York City. Businesspeople headed to work. The coffee and pastry stands on the city's street corners were doing a brisk business.*

*At 8:45 A.M., American Airlines Flight 11, hijacked by Mohammed Atta and four accomplices, slammed into the upper floors of the North Tower of the World Trade Center. Eighteen minutes later, United Airlines Flight 175, originally headed from Boston to Los Angeles, crashed into the South Tower. Thousands of gallons of highly flammable jet fuel ignited an inferno, and terrified workers fought their way through choking smoke and incredible heat in a desperate effort to escape.*

At 9:37 A.M., *American Airlines Flight 77, shortly after taking off from Virginia's Dulles International Airport, crashed into the Pentagon near Washington, D.C., and exploded. Smoke billowed from an enormous hole in the building's blackened outer wall.*

At about 10:00 A.M., *as the incinerating jet fuel melted steel support beams, the WTC's South Tower crumbled to the ground. Thousands of people ran through the streets of New York, followed by an enormous cloud of gray, ashy dust.*

At 10:10 A.M., *United Airlines Flight 93 from Newark, New Jersey, to San Francisco, California, crashed into an empty field near Pittsburgh, Pennsylvania. Appearing to be on a course for Washington, D.C., it may have been targeting the White*

Images of the wreckage of Flight 93 *(top)* and the gaping hole in the Pentagon *(above)* were seared onto Americans' minds on September 11.

*House for a suicide attack. The passengers on Flight 93, upon hearing via cell phones that other hijacked aircraft had been turned into guided bombs, confronted their hijackers, forcing their aircraft down and sacrificing their lives in a heroic attempt to spare others.*

*At 10:30 A.M., the North Tower of the World Trade Center also fell. The skyline of New York was forever altered.*

■ ■ ■ ■ ■ ■ ■ ■ ■ ■ ■ ■ ■ ■ ■ ■ ■ ■ ■ ■ ■ ■ ■ ■ ■ ■ ■ ■ ■ ■

Shortly after the hijackings, the Federal Aviation Administration shut down U.S. airspace to commercial traffic, and the closure very likely helped prevent other hijackers from taking off that morning. But the death toll from the September 11 attacks was still mind-boggling. The terrorists killed more than three thousand people from about fifty countries in the largest terrorist attack in U.S. history. September 11 was the day that America went to war.

## | THE WAR ON TERROR | The United States realized that a

regular war would never defeat al-Qaeda and other terrorist groups. No one government or nation represented terrorism. The nineteen September 11 hijackers had come from Saudi Arabia, Lebanon, Egypt, and Yemen, and they had trained at al-Qaeda facilities in Afghanistan. Underground al-Qaeda cells were scattered across the globe. Intelligence reports estimated that there were three thousand al-Qaeda operatives in Afghanistan, but thousands of sympathizers were scattered throughout the Middle East and beyond. Many of the group's leaders were unknown. In addition, al-Qaeda forces had assassinated Ahmad Shah Massoud— who might have been a powerful ally to the United States—just a few days before September 11. Clearly, the war could not target only the terrorists themselves. Their entire infrastructure—money, communications, and security—would have to be permanently disrupted.

One enemy was clear: the Taliban. Declaring a far-reaching War on Terror, the United States led an international coalition in an operation in Afghanistan. They bombed Taliban and al-Qaeda targets such as caves, training camps, and military installations in a relentless campaign.

One objective of the campaign in Afghanistan was the death or capture of bin Laden and his top lieutenants. Bombing attacks with that aim killed scores of al-Qaeda terrorists from about thirty nations, and the coalition forces captured and interrogated thousands more suspects. Many were flown under heavy guard to a detention facility at the U.S. base of Guantanamo Bay, Cuba.

U.S. special forces also searched the caves and tunnels of Afghanistan, where they found valuable evidence on al-Qaeda personnel, operations, and finances. The information gained from this seized evidence and from the interrogation of captured operatives revealed a frightening glimpse into al-Qaeda's plans for future strikes. These plans included assaults on U.S. targets around the world.

# TERRORIST GROUPS AFFILIATED WITH AL-QAEDA

Al-Qaeda's support of dozens of terrorist groups succeeded in creating a vast international network of terrorism, claiming volunteers from all over the globe. Among the groups believed to be in bin Laden's network are:

ALGERIA: FIS, GIA, and GSPC

BAHRAIN: Muslim Brotherhood

CHECHNYA, RUSSIA: Ibn al-Khattab's Afghan veterans and volunteers from the Saudi Wahhabi Movement

EGYPT: al-Jihad and al-Gamaa al-Islamiya

INDONESIA: Jemaah Islamiya

ISRAEL: Hamas and Palestinian Islamic Jihad

JORDAN: Muslim Brotherhood, Jaish-e-Muhammad (Army of Muhammad), and Bayat al-Imam (Homage to the Imam)

LEBANON: Hezbollah

LIBYA: Muslim Brotherhood and Fighting Islamic Group (FIG)

PAKISTAN: Harakat ul-Mujahideen (HUM), Hizb-ul-Mujahideen, Jamaat ul-Fuqra, and Lashkar-e-Taiba

THE PHILIPPINES: Abu Sayyaf Group

SAUDI ARABIA: Wahhabi Movement and Saudi Hezbollah

SYRIA: Muslim Brotherhood

TUNISIA: al-Nahda (Revival Movement)

TURKEY: Turkish Hezbollah

UZBEKISTAN: Islamic Movement of Uzbekistan

YEMEN: Islamic Army of Aden ■

U.S. forces deployed to Afghanistan in the War on Terror discover a store of arms in a remote cave. The weapons probably belonged to Taliban or al-Qaeda fighters.

| **AN UNENDING BATTLE** | The War on Terror went beyond Afghanistan. U.S. Special Forces were also sent to countries including Uzbekistan, Yemen, and the Philippines. But al-Qaeda proved to be a resilient foe. U.S. leaders had hoped that the international war against terrorism would cripple the group. Yet al-Qaeda survived the initial blitz in Afghanistan. Bin Laden's whereabouts—and whether or not he is even alive—are unknown. But al-Qaeda has managed to recover, regroup, and refinance its lethal underground army.

Although al-Qaeda remained largely inactive in the months following September 11, it launched renewed strikes in 2002. On April 11, 2002, a suicide bomber drove a truck into an ancient synagogue on the Tunisian island of Jerba, killing five people. In May 2002, FBI agents arrested al-Qaeda operative Jose Padilla at O'Hare Airport in Chicago after Padilla had flown in from Pakistan. He was suspected of planning to bomb a U.S. city with a "dirty bomb"—a bomb with radioactive material packed around it. Attacks continued in the following autumn. On October 6, 2002, al-Qaeda terrorists sailing in small skiffs laden with explosives detonated themselves alongside the *Limburg*, a French oil tanker near the Yemeni coast. Seventeen crewmembers were wounded, and one was killed. The ship caught fire and began leaking oil. Just a few days later, al-Qaeda would strike again, in a far-reaching and lethal attack.

## Terror in Paradise

**On October 12, 2002,** *Bali's nightclubs were busy, as usual. Thousands of tourists flocked to the Indonesian island each year, and that night the Kuta Beach area was filled with people enjoying the mild weather and the popular clubs.*

*Just before midnight, the explosion of a suicide car bomb shook one of the crowded clubs, filling it with screams, smoke, and debris. As people fled the scene, a second, larger blast tore through the nearby Sari Club, followed several minutes later by an explosion at the U.S. consulate two miles away. In all, more than 180 men, women, and children were killed, and hundreds more were injured.*

The twisted shells of cars litter the scene of the
Bali bombings.

*Investigators soon connected al-Qaeda to the Bali attack, believing that it may have been carried out with the cooperation of the Jemaah Islamiya, an Islamic extremist group in Southeast Asia that has ties to al-Qaeda.*

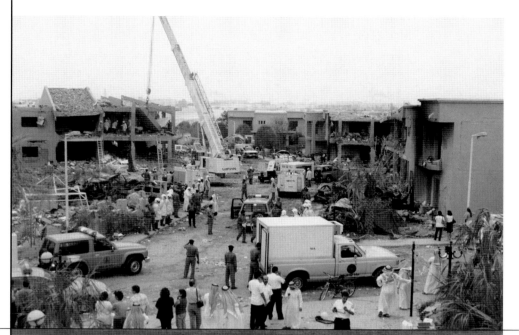

The attack on this Riyadh, Saudi Arabia, housing complex—inhabited mostly by Americans and other foreign workers—served as a violent reminder that al-Qaeda is still active.

The Bali attacks were followed by a period of relative quiet, as the wave of attacks seemed to have slowed. However, experts warned that al-Qaeda was far from gone, as it still claimed an estimated eighteen thousand operatives in more than seventy-five nations around the world. At the same time, the War on Terror continued. In the first few months of 2003, U.S. and Pakistani forces captured several high-ranking al-Qaeda members, including the chief of operations Khalid Shaikh Mohammed and a lieutenant named Tawfiq Attash Khallad. But the quiet was shattered in May 2003 by a series of suicide bombings in Saudi Arabia and Morocco, proving that al-Qaeda remains a powerful and deadly force.

# EPILOGUE*

Although the War on Terror has had some victories, funding and support for terrorism still flourish. Western actions in the Arab and Muslim world, in particular, give fundamentalist groups new momentum. For example, a U.S.-led war against Iraq in March and April 2003 provoked new resentment and hostility against U.S. presence in the region.

## AL-JIHAD AND AL-GAMAA AL-ISLAMIYA

Most of Egypt's terrorism movements have joined the al-Qaeda network and no longer carry out many operations on their own. These members of bin Laden's global organization represent a serious threat. One of the leaders of the September 11 attacks was Egyptian.

## HEZBOLLAH

In April 2003, a suicide bomber believed to be a Hezbollah member struck a café in Tel Aviv, Israel, killing three and wounding more than fifty. Lebanese leaders say that they are committed to stopping terrorism. However, some officials in Lebanon, Syria, and Iran still support Hezbollah, claiming that it is not truly a terrorist group but a justified resistance movement to Israeli authority in the region.

## GIA AND SALAFIST GROUP FOR PREACHING AND COMBAT (GSPC)

In January 2003, GIA operatives attacked two families in northern Algeria, killing thirteen. The GIA often targets civilians. In late February or early March 2003, members of the GIA splinter organization GSPC took thirty-two European travelers hostage in Algeria. Algerian commandos rescued seventeen of the hostages in May 2003, but the other fifteen remain captive.

## AL-QAEDA

On May 12, 2003, nine terrorists believed to be associated with al-Qaeda detonated suicide bombs outside three housing developments in Riyadh, Saudi Arabia. The attack, aimed primarily at Westerners, killed more than twenty people. The attack was the first connected with al-Qaeda in several months, but another followed on May 16 in Casablanca, Morocco. Authorities worry that these strikes may signal an upsurge in al-Qaeda violence.

*Please note that the information contained in this book was current at the time of publication. To find sources for late-breaking news, please consult the websites listed on page 69.

# TIMELINE

| |
|---|
| Egyptian groups |
| Lebanese groups |
| Algerian groups |
| Al-Qaeda |
| General |

ca. 610 C.E.    Muhammad founds Islam in Mecca.

622    Muhammad and his followers flee to Medina, where the new religion flourishes.

691    The Dome of the Rock, one of Islam's holiest sites, is built in Jerusalem.

1096-1270    The Crusades take place.

1300s    The Ottoman Empire emerges.

1400s-1500s    The Ottoman Empire reaches its greatest power.

1800s    European nations found colonies in former Ottoman holdings.

1914-1918    World War I takes place. After the war, Great Britain, France, and other victors divide much of the remaining Ottoman Empire among themselves.

1922    Egypt gains independence from Britain.

1928    Hasan al-Banna founds the Muslim Brotherhood in Egypt.

1939    World War II begins.

1943    Lebanon wins its independence from France.

1945    World War II ends. Thousands of Holocaust survivors emigrate to British-controlled Palestine.

1948    The Jewish State of Israel is created. Muslim Brotherhood members assassinate Egypt's prime minister.

1954    Algeria's war of independence begins.

1962    Algeria wins its independence from France.

1967    The Six-Day War takes place.

late 1960s    Al-Jihad takes shape, led by Sheikh Omar Abdel Rahman.

1970s    An oil boom widens the gap between rich and poor in much of the Middle East.

1973    The Yom Kippur War takes place.

1975    Civil war erupts in Lebanon.

1977    Egyptian president Anwar el-Sadat begins peace talks with Israel.

1978    Israel invades Lebanon, targeting Palestinian militants there.

1979    The Ayatollah Kuhollah Khomeini takes power in an Islamic revolution in Iran. Soviet troops invade Afghanistan.

1980s    Abdullah Yusuf Azzam and Osama bin Laden organize mujahideen to fight the Soviets in Afghanistan.

1981    Anwar el-Sadat is assassinated by al-Jihad.

1982    Israel invades Lebanon. Christian militias carry out massacres at the Sabra and Shatila refugee camps. Hezbollah is formed.

1983    Hezbollah carries out several suicide bombings against Western targets in the Middle East.

1985    Hezbollah operatives hijack TWA Flight 847.

1989    Al-Qaeda takes shape.

1990    Iraq invades Kuwait. U.S. troops enter Saudi Arabia.

1991    The Islamic Salvation Front (FIS) wins major victories in Algerian elections.

1992    The Algerian military cancels national elections expected to be won by the FIS. The Armed Islamic Group (GIA) is formed.

1993    Al-Jihad operatives make assassination attempts on two high-ranking Egyptian officials. An al-Qaeda team led by Ramzi Yousef bombs the World Trade Center.

1994  GIA operatives hijack Air France Flight 8969, planning to crash it into the Eiffel Tower.

1995  Al-Gamaa al-Islamiya members attempt to assassinate Egyptian president Hosni Mubarak. Al-Qaeda is connected to the bombing of a U.S. military barracks in Saudi Arabia.

1996  Al-Qaeda is suspected of a second bombing of a military barracks in Saudi Arabia. Bin Laden and al-Qaeda relocate from Sudan to Afghanistan, where they are supported by the Taliban.

1997  Al-Gamaa al-Islamiya attacks tourists in the Valley of the Kings, killing sixty-five. The Islamic Salvation Army (AIS) signs a cease-fire with the Algerian government.

1998  The Salafist Group for Preaching and Combat (GSPC) becomes more active in Algerian terrorism. Al-Qaeda operatives bomb two U.S. embassies in Africa. Bin Laden forms the World Islamic Front for Jihad against Jews and Crusaders.

2000  Al-Qaeda bombers strike the USS *Cole* while it is docked in Aden, Yemen.

2001  The attacks of September 11 take place. The United States declares a War on Terror. U.S.-led coalition forces bomb al-Qaeda and Taliban targets in Afghanistan.

2002  Al-Qaeda operatives bomb the *Limburg*, a French ship off the Yemeni coast. Bombers believed to be working with al-Qaeda strike nightclubs in Bali.

2003  A U.S.-led war against Iraq raises fears of renewed anti-Western hostility and terrorism. Westerners in Riyadh, Saudi Arabia, and Casablanca, Morocco, are targeted by suicide bombings believed to be directed by al-Qaeda.

# SELECTED BIBLIOGRAPHY

Alexander, Yonah, and Michael S. Swetman. *Usama bin Laden's al-Qaida: Profile of a Terrorist Network*. Ardsley, NY: Transnational Publishers, Inc., 2001.

Baer, Robert. *See No Evil: The True Story of a Ground Soldier in the CIA's War on Terrorism*. New York: Crown Publishing, 2002.

Bergen, Peter L. *Holy War, Inc.: Inside the Secret World of Osama bin Laden*. New York: The Free Press, 2001.

Bodansky, Yosef. *Bin Laden: The Man Who Declared War on America*. New York: Prima Publishing, 1999.

Cooley, John K. *Payback: America's Long War in the Middle East*. McLean, VA: Brassey's US, 1991.

Dietl, Wilhelm. *Holy War*. New York: MacMillan, 1984.

Emerson, Steve. *American Jihad: The Terrorists Living among Us*. New York: Free Press, 2002.

Esposito, John L. *Unholy War: Terror in the Name of Islam*. Oxford, UK: Oxford University Press, 2002.

Gunartatna, Rohan. *Inside Al Qaeda*. New York: Columbia University Press, 2002.

Jaber, Hala. *Hezbollah*. New York: Columbia University Press, 1997.

Katz, Samuel M. *Relentless Pursuit: The DSS and the Manhunt for the al-Qaeda Terrorists*. New York: Forge Press, 2002.

Pipes, Daniel. *Militant Islam Reaches America*. New York: W.W. Norton and Company, 2002.

Rashid, Ahmed. *Jihad: The Rise of Militant Islam in Central Asia*. New Haven, CT: Yale University Press, 2002.

Reeve, Simon. *The New Jackals: Ramzi Yousef, Osama bin Laden and the Future of Terrorism*. Boston: Northeastern University Press, 1999.

Sa'ad-Ghorayeb, Amal. *Hizbu'llah: Politics and Religion*. Critical Studies on Islam Series. London: Pluto Press, 2002.

Weaver, Mary Anne. *A Portrait of Egypt: A Journey Through the World of Militant Islam*. New York: Farrar, Straus and Giroux, 1999.

Wright, Robin B. *The Last Great Revolution: Turmoil and Transformation in Iran*. New York: Vintage, 2000.

———. *Sacred Rage: The Wrath of Militant Islam*. New York: Touchstone Books, 2001.

# FURTHER READING AND WEBSITES

**Books**

Behnke, Alison. *Afghanistan in Pictures.* Minneapolis, MN: Lerner Publications Company, 2003.

Currie, Stephen. *Terrorists and Terrorist Groups.* San Diego: Lucent Books, 2002.

Fridell, Ron. *Terrorism: Political Violence at Home and Abroad.* Berkeley Heights, NJ: Enslow Publishers, 2001.

Katz, Samuel M. *Jerusalem or Death: Palestinian Terrorism.* Minneapolis, MN: Lerner Publications Company, 2004.

Marcovitz, Hal. *Terrorism.* Philadelphia: Chelsea House Publishers, 2001.

Taus-Bolstad, Stacy. *Iran in Pictures.* Minneapolis, MN: Lerner Publications Company, 2004.

Taylor, Robert. *The History of Terrorism.* San Diego: Lucent Books, 2002.

Woolf, Alex. *Osama bin Laden.* Minneapolis, MN: Lerner Publications Company, 2004.

Zuehlke, Jeffrey. *Egypt in Pictures.* Minneapolis, MN: Lerner Publications Company, 2003.

**Websites**

*BBC News World Edition*
<http://news.bbc.co.uk/>
This website provides extensive coverage of international news, along with an in-depth look at Islamic fundamentalist activities.

*The Center for Defense Information: Terrorism Project*
<http://www.cdi.org/terrorism>
This website provides detailed articles on a variety of topics related to terrorism.

*CNN.com*
<http://www.cnn.com>
This news site is a source of breaking news on terrorism and other world events. It also offers a searchable archive of past articles.

*The New York Times on the Web*
<http://www.nytimes.com>
Access current *New York Times* articles on terrorism and terrorist groups at this site, or search the archive for older materials.

*Terrorism Questions and Answers*
<http://www.terrorismanswers.com>
This website, operated by the Markle Foundation (a nonprofit group that studies communications and media), presents a wealth of information through question-and-answer sheets on various aspects of terrorism.

*The Terrorism Research Center*
<http://www.homelandsecurity.com>
This comprehensive site offers profiles of terrorist groups, timelines of terrorist activity, and more.

*U.S. Department of State Counterterrorism Office*
<http://www.state.gov/s/ct>
This site, maintained by the U.S. government, provides information on terrorist groups and their activities.

# INDEX

# ABOUT THE AUTHOR

Samuel M. Katz is an expert in the field of international terrorism and counterterrorism, military special operations, and law enforcement. He has written more than twenty books and dozens of articles on these subjects, as well as creating documentaries and giving lectures. Mr. Katz also serves as editor in chief of *Special Ops*, a magazine dedicated to the discussion of special operations around the world, and observes counterterrorism and special operations units in action in Europe and the Middle East. The Terrorist Dossiers series is his first foray into the field of nonfiction for young people.

# PHOTO ACKNOWLEDGMENTS

The images in this book are used with the permission of: © NYPP/ZUMA Press, p. 8; © TRIP/TRIP, p. 11; © TRIP/H ROGERS, p. 12; © Archivo Iconografico, S.A./CORBIS, p. 13; Cultural and Tourism Office of the Turkish Embassy, p. 14; Kluger Zoltan/State of Israel National Photo Collection, p. 15; © Peter Turnley/CORBIS, pp. 17, 27; AP/Wide World Photos, pp. 20, 21, 25 (bottom), 26, 28, 51; State of Israel National Photo Collection, p. 22; © AFP/CORBIS, pp. 23, 33, 34, 46, 52, 58 (top), 63; Saar Yaacov/State of Israel National Photo Collection, p. 24; © Kevin Fleming/CORBIS, p. 25 (top); © Hulton Archive, pp. 30, 41; © Bettmann/CORBIS, pp. 31, 32, 35, 40; © Action Press/ZUMA Press, p. 37; © Reuters NewMedia Inc./CORBIS, pp. 38, 49, 53, 55, 62; © GYORI ANTOINE/CORBIS SYGMA, pp. 42, 43; © Gabriel Bouys/AFP/Getty Images, p. 44; © CORBIS SYGMA, p. 45; © Getty Images, Getty Images North America, p. 47; © Reza/Webistan/CORBIS, p. 48; © MAIMAN RICK/CORBIS SYGMA, p. 54; © Liz Gilbert/CORBIS SYGMA, p. 56; © Isaac Menashe/Zuma Press, p. 58 (bottom); United States Navy Photo, p. 61. Maps on pp. 16, 19, 29, and 39 by Laura Westlund. Cover © Maher Attar/CORBIS SYGMA.